MUSTANG

An American Classic

TEXT AND PHOTOGRAPHS BY

Nicky Wright

TODTRI

DEDICATION
For Sharon, Julian, Ambre, Britainy, and David, the best kiddies anyone could have.

ACKNOWLEDGMENTS
The author would like to thank the following individuals and companies for their
advice and for allowing their cars to be photographed for this book: Tom and Carol Podemski,
Don and Tom and Judy Bergman, Ford Motor Company, John Clor, DanReid, Craig Atkins,
Ford SVT, Elaine Hopkins, Ford Press Vehicles, Mike Barron & Luis Corona, Rod Butler,
Chuck Edwards, Ronald, Robbie, Renea and Rick Miller, Auburn-Cord-Duesenberg Museum,
Mark Dollier, Walt & Marilyn Wise, Lonnie Krag, Campbell Advertising, Dearborn, MI.,
Mike Barron and Luis Corona, Dennis Begley, Steve Turland, Fuji Films, Pentax Cameras, and
Nikon Cameras. All photographs in this book were taken with either Pentax or Nikon cameras.

This book was designed and produced by
TODTRI Book Publishers
P.O. Box 572, New York, NY 10116-0572
FAX: (212) 695-6984

Printed and bound in China

ISBN 1-57717-082-2

Author: Nicky Wright

Publisher: Robert M. Tod
Editor: Edward Douglas
Assistant Editor: Don Kennison
Designer: Mark Weinberg
Typesetting: Command-O Design

Photo Credits

Contents

Index

Introduction

As we cross the threshold into the twenty-first century, those of us of a certain age may take a last, longing glance back to the good old days—our good old days. For us, they were in the fabulous fifties and the swinging sixties. Many of us, like most youngsters in those days, followed the Beatles, the Rolling Stones, Bob Dylan, and Jane Fonda's *Barbarella*, and we knew about and were captivated by the Mustang.

So was the San Francisco truck driver on April 17, 1964, when the Mustang was first unveiled for all the world to see. So taken by the cute little car in the Ford dealer's showroom, the mesmerized trucker drove his rig through the showroom window, obviously intent on being the first to see the new motoring sensation. The idea behind the Mustang was brilliant: to restore the pleasure of motoring that had been taken away by giant cars equipped with every convenience. While only the rich could afford a Ferrari or Aston Martin, here now was a car that even a struggling college student could save for.

Ford Division president Lee Iacocca's little black book contained the idea that became the Mustang. He had a sixth sense that a small, sporty, inexpensive car with a low base price, a long list of options, and engines with real get-up-and-go, would appeal to the young. He was right. The first eighteen months of production broke all records and sent the rest of the auto industry into a frenzy. From the first day onward, the name Mustang has evoked an instant response.

People have fond memories of the Mustang, because it was a car that truly belonged to the generation it was designed for. There were the boulevard cruising Mustangs with six-cylinder engines—at best a 289 two-barrel—or the Hollywood and Vine rip roaring, gut wrenching 302s, 390s and 428s. They handled and stopped better than most, and Carroll Shelby nurtured them into race winning, blood-and-thunder machines.

But no matter what, Mustang had in the beginning—and still has to this day—one element that is missing from most cars: charisma. A Mustang, old or new, has an inescapable pull. One wants get in and drive it. Try the latest Cobra SAT, and you will see that the magic is still there. This book

The beginning of a legend. Launched on April 17th 1964, the Mustang was the quintessential

*Lee Iacocca was the genius behind the fabled
Mustang. Without Iacocca, Ford might not
have been in the strong position it is today.*

CHAPTER ONE

The Tale from the Little Black Book

The year 1959 was a good one. It was the final year of a prosperous decade that sowed the roots of change. This great decade of plenty was reflected in the cars America drove and loved. Big, fat, finny, and flashy, with 350 horsepower under the hood, this was the type of car that Detroit gave to a motor hungry nation. Then, the fickle public's taste began to change, and by the end of the decade many people were buying Volkswagen Beetles. Except for American Motors with its Rambler American, and struggling Studebaker with the Lark, few auto makers thought that small cars would appeal to suburban America. However, with the introduction of compact cars, the independents scored mightily and soared up the sales charts.

The Big Three scrambled to follow suit with their own smaller models. Of these, the conventional and conservative Ford Falcon, with its simple design, was the most popular. People were turning away from triple colors and chrome, and wanted smaller cars with straightforward engines. The success of the Falcon, which sold more cars than all other compacts put together, was largely due to Ford Division president, Robert McNamara, who was interested in the bottom line, and had changed Ford's direction to ensure profitability.

Iacocca's Vision

When McNamara left the company in 1961 to join the administration of President John F. Kennedy, he was succeeded by Lee Iacocca, a young man who had risen meteorically in the ranks to become vice-president of the Ford Division at the age of thirty-six. From the start, Iacocca sought to make changes, believing that the youth market would ensure the continued profitability established by McNamara. He knew that the baby boomers—those born after World War II—would soon be the nation's consumers.

Iacocca understood that the new generation would want excitement in style as well as power under the hood. He envisioned a small, sporty

FOLLOWING PAGE: Available with the 289-cubic-inch V-8 rated at 225 or 271 horsepower, the 1965 Mustang GT first appeared late in the season. It was well received and gave a true indication that Mustang was a force to be reckoned with.

An old man and his dynasty. Henry Ford, left, in one of those awkward, very posed pictures with his son, Edsel (center) and grandson, Henry Ford II. Henry the Second ousted his grandfather in what might be termed a government inspired coup.

car with enough options to give it individual expression, and a base price of around $2,300.

As he developed his plans, he jotted down his ideas and observations in a little black book, which he always carried with him to record his thoughts as they occured.

Reflecting on the staid, conventional McNamara legacy, Iacocca knew that something had to be done to create a new and youthful image for Ford. With the baby boomers in mind, he initiated the Total Performance Program, which returned Ford to racing, whipping up a storm on the NASCAR ovals with stylish fastback Galaxies. In Europe, Ford won with the compact Falcon in the prestigious Monte Carlo Rally, and then moved on to the world's greatest road race, the Le Mans 24 Hour event.

Having caught the attention of the younger generation, Iacocca presented his idea for a sporty, four-seater, small car to Ford executives. He was bolstered by market research which showed that the age 15 to 29 segment of the population would grow by fifty percent within the next ten years. Furthermore, a survey of people under the age of twenty-five indicated strong interest in an affordable car that offered four-speed manual transmission, bucket seats, optional engines, and sporty good looks.

The interior of a 1965 Mustang Fastback displays the sporty nature of design. Note the fake steering wheel spokes.

Getting It Right

Though it wasn't hard to decide to build such a car, designing it was another matter. At first it seemed that the first try, known as Mustang I, would be a success. It was a two seater, like the Triumph and MG, and was an instant hit with racing drivers and the automotive press. It was not a hit, however, with Lee Iacocca. He insisted that Mustang I was too expensive to build, and since it was impractical as a family car, would not be popular with the general public.

More evidence was coming through that the babyboomers wanted four seats, not two. A new concept had to be designed. To ensure he got what he wanted, Iacocca assigned all of FoMoCo's design teams in a competition to see who would build the right car. With four separate design studios working night and day, the styling teams prepared seven different clay models for evaluation. In the end, it was the design Ford Styling's Dave Ash that won the day. Ash's car was based on the Falcon floorpan, had a 108-inch wheelbase and 186-inch overall length, six inches longer than the specifications called for. This would be corrected in the production version. Actually there was very little modification to Ash's original design.

Since V-8 powerplants were popular, the Mustang II was designed to take both six-cylinder and V-8 engines. As it turned out, the six was the entry or standard engine, but the great majority of buyers opted for the range of V-8s Mustangs would have up until 1973. Soon the car was ready, and the production lines tooled up.

The Mustang Arrives

Just prior to its public introduction on April 17, 1964, the Mustang was the subject of a massive media campaign, with cover stories in both *Time* and *Newseek*, prime time commercials on all three television networks, and articles and

dvertisements in 2,600 newspapers. So succesful was this coverage, that on he first day the dealers hardly knew what hit them. They were expecting crowd, but nothing like the stampede that occurred.

A Chicago dealer became so worried, that he locked his showroom doors prevent people getting crushed in the melee. Another dealer placed a shiny ew Mustang up on a grease rack and raised it above the crowd, so all could e it without damaging the car or themselves. There were even people so ager to buy a Mustang that they were willing to pay much more than the tandard price. Realizing this, a Garland, Texas dealer held an impromptu uction and had fifteen people bidding for his sole Mustang. He sold it to the ighest bidder, who stayed in the car all night while his check cleared to make ure the car wasn't sold in his absence.

It goes without saying that the Mustang was a phenomenal success. No car, efore or since, ever caused such excitement. As to whether the car was worth ll the fuss, the answer has to be yes. At the time there was nothing else on he market quite like it. It bubbled over with attractive good looks and had a efinite personality. Initially there were two models, a coupe and convertible. 2 + 2 fastback came a little later in the year. The car was decidedly hand-ome, its long hood and short deck design complementing European cars.

Here is the 2 + 2 Mustang Fastback. It was first introduced in September 1964, some six months after the coupe and convertible.

Up front, the narrow, bluish grey honeycomb grille was framed by a three-sided chrome strip and featured the chrome plate galloping pony in its center. Obviously fake air scoops flanked either side of the grille, and it is here that the Mustang was let down by poor design and quality. The squarish headlight bezels were separate units. as were the fake scoops, and rarely did the pieces match each other or the fenders. Most motoring journals noticed the problem and said so, sometimes in very unforgiving terms. Ford took notice and the offending pieces were redesigned and made as one in 1967.

The Basic Mustang

Iacocca wanted the Mustang to have a huge list of options to encourage buyers to individualize their cars. This was so successful that there are hardly two Mustangs exactly alike. For instance, with the wheel covers there was a standard set and five optional ones. The standard wheels were 13-inches in diameter, and had a bead width of 4 inches. Fourteen-inch wheels were standard with the handling package.

Front and rear bumpers were slim and nicely styled, but useless a collision. They were set against the body metal and offered little or no protection. The sides had unique sculpturing. The scooped appearance began as a line from the beginning of the front fender, and continued and became more pronounced as it ended in front of the rear wheel arch. Here, the scoop curved acutely downward and was finished off by a simulated air intake. Then the scooped indentation came back on itself, finishing just behind the front wheel opening, just below the Mustang pony emblem mounted on a red, white, and blue slim vertical bar. Three vertical chrome bars mounted together, covered the tail lights

Apart from revised, simulated rear-quarter air scoops and the absence of the chrome bars in the grille, the 1966 Mustang hardtop coupe is identical to the 1965 model. This particular car has the standard I-6 engine.

either side. Though they appeared to be three separate lights, they were actually one unit, cleverly designed to give the appearance of three. In the center of the car's rear was the very attractive chrome gas cap, with its thermal embossed Mustang emblem encased within.

The interior was very handsome and quite expensive looking. All-vinyl bucket seats were standard equipment, with bench front seats as an was option that was hardly ever seen. The rear seat was a bench type. A molded plastic instrument panel made of plastic chrome with white-on-black numbers was standard, though there was an optional "Rally Pac" which consisted of two circular dials on either side of the steering column. The speedometer was horizontal and flanked by round dials showing temperature and gas gauges. The Rally Pac consisted of tachometer and clock. A crash pad was standard atop the instrument panel.

Under the hood, the standard engine was a 170-cubic-inch six-cylinder unit developing 101 brake horsepower (bhp). A six-cylinder equipped Mustang was capable of 90 miles per hour (mph). If the wind conditions were right, it was possible to reach 80 mph in 35 seconds. There were two V-8s, the 260-cubic-inch unit boasting 160 bhp, and the 289-cubic-inch displacement (cid) with 200 bhp. Later would come a high performance 289 pushing out 271 bhp. All the V-8s were healthy performers, the 271 horse version especially so. New production records were set by the Mustang. It became a love affair between man—woman too—and machine.

The Price Was Right

Between April 1964 and September 1965, Ford sold a whopping 619,243 Mustangs. Of this total, 418,812 were snapped up in the first twelve months. Its immediate acceptance was unparalleled in the history of the automobile, and Lee Iacocca's vision had proved to be right. As for the affordable price, a six-cylinder base Mustang—without frills—left the showroom for a mere $2,372, and the V-8 equipped version sold for only $2,480. The list of options could hike the price to almost $4,000, though probably not many people went that far. Most cars sold for an estimated average of $3,250.

Among the options were such items as power steering at $86.30, power brakes for $43.20, and center console for $51.50. A radio and antenna would add $58, and air conditioning—a must in some regions—was priced at $238.20. Initially, front disc brakes were optional and cost $58. If a buyer chose all of these options, the addional cost wooould be $535,20, bringing the total price of a V-8 Mustang to $3,015.

Another way to obtain options was to buy them in groups. For instance the Handling Package would provide heavy duty suspension and shock absorbers, larger diameter front stabiliser bar, and a 22-to-1 steering ratio. Then for extra interior pizzazz, there was the Interior Decor Group which offered padded sun visors, wood- grain. applique ornamentation, a five-dial instrument cluster, a deluxe wood-grain steering wheel, and red and white door courtesy lights. All of this, including radio, air conditioning, power steering, and power disc brakes would have brought the grand total for a V-8 to $3,188.

The motoring press, dismayed by Ford's rejection of the advanced Mustang I, had scant praise for the Mustang when it was introduced. One magazine called it "a nice looking Falcon," while another dismissed it as "little more than another Detroit compact." But no matter what the journals said, people still loved the Mustang.

Improving Performance

In September 1964, Ford introduced the Mustang fastback 2 + 2. Not only was it beautiful to look at, but practical as well. The rear seat folded down to create a huge, fully carpeted luggage area capable of carrying such things as surfboards, small ladders, a full complement of suitcases, and more besides. Equipped with the High Performanc 271 bhp, 289 V-8, introduced in June 1964, road tests of the fastback realized 0–60 times of 8.3 seconds, and a halfway decent quarter-mile time of 15.9 seconds at 85 mph. Compression ratio of the new engine was 10.5: 1.

Speaking of the high performance V-8, Ford initiated other engine changes The 260 cid, 164 horse V-8 disappeared in the fall of 1964 to be replaced by a 200 hp 289. Also replaced was the 170-cubic-inch, 101 bhp standard six. The new six displaced 200 cubic-inches and developed 120 hp.

In Fall 1965, Ford decided it needed to create even more of a performance image around the Mustang to bring it more in line with the company's Total Performance Program, which was paying healthy dividends in competition and, ultimately, in sales. Other manufacturers were jumping onto the performance bandwagon. There was the Chevrolet 409 and the intermediate Dodge and Plymouth cars, powered with a second generation 426-cubic-inch hemi, that won race after race on the NASCAR ovals.

The Shelby Mustang

However, it was the Corvette, America's only true sports car, that Ford decided to challenge. To do this, the company went to the one man who could create miracles in the sporting world, Carroll Shelby, creator of the fabulous A.C. Shelby Cobra. He agreed to build a high performance Mustang that coul be homolongated for racing.

There were unique differences that separated the finished Shelby Mustang from the standard production cars. First and foremost was the engine and mechanicals. Shelby specified the 289 High Performance engine which was given a better breathing, Cobra aluminum high-rise intake manifold, finned cast aluminum valve covers, and finned aluminum oilpan. A special Holley center-pivotfloat, four- barrel carburetor, and steel tube Tri-Y exhaust headers completed the picture. Glass- packed, bullet mufflers were used with the exhaust pipes that exited forward of the rear wheels. The 271 bhp V-8 developed 306 horses, once the Shelby team had done their magic.

To save weight, a glass fiber hood with a functional hood scoop was employed, and a grille without the chrome running-pony emblem. Racing style hood pins were standard fare. A racing stripe designated GT350 at the beginning, just behind the front wheel well, continued along the rocker panel: to the rear wheel well. Wide twin racing stripes started at the front valence and ran over the hood and roof, ending on the rear deck.

All 1965 Shelby Mustangs featured a small horse and bar on the driver's side of the grille. The racing stripes were a dealer installed option, and came in a Guardsman Blue color only. The Shelby Mustangs were painted white in the beginning, with interiors only in black. A one-piece fiberglass shelf covered the area where the rear seat would have been and acted as a mount for the spare tire. Unlike the deeply dished Ford Mustang steering wheel, the Shelby version was flat with a wooden rim. Three-inch competition seat belts were standard.

The heart of the matter, the Shelby modified 289 High Performance V-8. It developed 306 bhp, and had unique Shelby pieces, such as an aluminum Cobra intake manifold among other goodies.

In contrast to the 13- or 14-inch wheels on the standard Mustang, Shelby Mustangs came with 15 inch-wheels shod in Blue Dot 7.75 x 15-inch tires. An option was the special five-spoke, an aluminum wheel built by Cragar to Shelby specifications.

A very nice view showing off the 1965 Mustang Fastback in all its glory.

The Right Car

Drivers and road testers trying out the Shelby Mustang for the first time realized they were in something special. Zero to 60 was accomplished in 6.8 seconds, and quicker steering helped the tight, responsive handling, which sacrificed comfort for a harsh, jittery ride on rough road surfaces.

As noted earlier, Ford asked Shelby to improve the Mustang's image with both street and racing cars. If anything, the race cars were mind blowing. The 289 cid engines were stretched to 340-360 bhp and won every race in sight. They were built to compete against Corvettes inthe Sports Car Club of America (SCCA) B-Production class ,which the GT350s virtually dominated. Only thirty of the 562 Shelby GT350 units built in 1965 were racing models. The standard GT350 retailed for $4,500, while the racing model was priced at $5,950. Carroll Shelby had worked his magic, and Mustang's image climbed to new heights.There is little doubt that the new Mustang was the right car for the right time.

Ford was dancing all the way to the bank, having reached a record 619,243 production figure for a new model. There were very few changes in the 1966 model. A neater rear scoop replaced the tinny 1965 units, and there were redesigned chrome-styled steel wheels. An extruded aluminum, eggcrate grille replaced the honeycomb of 1965. Now the pony and corral were suspended in

ace, because the vertical and horizontal chrome bars holding the corral had been removed, aking the car more sporty.

Another slight change was the thin chrome strip added to the hood lip. It had been offered only n GT models in 1965, but was standard across the range in 1966. As for the interior, the dashboard as redesigned to have a single dial, flanked on either side by two smaller ones. Special handling nd performance packages continued into 1966. For those who wanted real pep, there was the GT Mustang , and for brazen muscle, the 1966 Shelby Mustang. It was mostly held over from 1965, ut the exhausts now exited from the rear instead of from the sides of the car. A rear seat was ade available, Ford's C-4 automatic transmission was offered, and the car could be ordered in five ifferent colors. To cut production costs, certain mechanical niceties, such as lowering the upper -arms and fitting over-ride torque arms, were stopped.

Hertz-Rent-A-Car was very interested in the Shelby GT350 Mustang. So much so, that they rdered 1,000 special units that would be offered as part of Hertz's rental fleet. These cars would o into the Hertz Sportscar Club, and be offered to enthusiasts. In the end, 936 cars were delivered. lmost all were black with gold stripes, though a few were painted such colors as metallic red. ome early cars had the four-speed manual transmission, but all later ones came with the C4 utomatic. Due to the Hertz order, 1966 Shelby Mustang production hit 2,380 units.

Special Editions

n 1966, Ford sold its millionth Mustang, quite a feat for a car barely two years old. To promote he event, Ford brought out a one-year-only, special edition Mustang. Called the Sprint, the model as powered by the 200 cid six-cylinder engine with a chrome air cleaner marked with a Mustang owered Sprint 200 decal. Apart from the inclusion of a few optional extras, the Sprint was identi- al to any other 6-cylinder Mustang. Nevertheless, the hype worked, and the Sprint sold.

Even more limited was the Playboy Pink Mustang. *Playboy* magazine ordered a few Mustang onvertibles, all painted a unique Playboy Pink. When the cars were delivered in this feminine ue, they were used by the magazine for promotional purposes.

Of interest is the Mustang exported to Germany. While it was the same as U.S. versions, it was nown in that country as the T-5, since its name conflicted with a German company called Mustang. here aren't too many T-5 models around, and probably most of those left are still in Europe.

The five-lug, five-spoke wheel was a sporty and attractive option for 1966 Mustangs. Shelby versions had the cobra emblem in the center rather than the pony.

. very rare and curious Mustang. Painted Playboy ink, only a few units of this ar were made. It has a rumble eat built into the trunk, though ot a very practical one. The car as custom built, but never took off.

Facing Competition

Since Mustang dominated the pony car field, other companies began to design cars that would offer a challenge to Ford's success. Aware of this, Ford ordered a redesign of the Mustang for l967 to iron out problems encountered in the previous two and a half years. What resulted was an automobile superior to the previous models. In addition, the Mustang engine line-up increased by one with the addition of Thunderbird's 390-cubic inch V-8. Now there were three 289 V-8s, the standard six-cylinder, and the new 390, which developed 320 bhp. Length was increased from 181.6 to 183.6 inches, and width grew from 68.2 to 70.9 inches to accomodate the 390 engine.

Of note was the larger grille and the return of the horizontal and vertical bars holding the pony and corral in the center. The rectangular mesh grille was set further back and surrounded on all sides by a bright metal strip, providing a simpler, cleaner appearance. The headlight rims and outer grille sides were all one piece, and the fake louvers on either side of the 1965–66 grille were eliminated. Side sculpturing remained but was deeper, ending in a pair of useless, color-keyed scoops in front of the rear wheel well. The rear was concave and contained the single tail lights split into three sections by the chrome bezels.

New on the convertibles was a folding, glass, rear window. Inside the car, the new interior boasted a nicely re-styled dashboard, consisting of two large dials and three smaller ones set almost flush with the dashboard face. There was Selectaire air conditioning and

In 1966, Hertz-Rent-a-Car asked Carroll Shelby to build 1,000 special Mustangs similar to the Mustang Shelby GT-350. Shelby happily obliged, and the result was the GT-350H. The "H" stands for Hertz.

etter designed seats. Already aware of the Federal Government's restless insistence on safer automobiles, Ford made seat belts standard and gave the Mustang a deeply dished steering wheel with a heavily padded center hub.

Although the same three body styles; coupe, convertible, and fastback remained, there was a new model: the GT-A, with A standing for automatic. Built as a one-year-only model, it came with the 390 V-8, GT Equipment Group and Interior Decor Option. In a straight line, the GT-A could do 0–60 in around 7.5 seconds. The car was incredibly fast in a straight line, but its front-end overweight bias prevented it from whizzing around corners. Superior handling was available with the 289 Hi-Po engine, since it was lighter in weight.

Another model was the limited edition Pacesetter Special. This coupe model, with dual-tape stripes running the length of the car above the side sculpturing, was built to coincide with the Indianapolis 500, which Ford thought Mustang would pace, but in the end, did not.

Shelby made some revolutionary changes in the 1967 Shelby Mustang. He extended its length three inches over the standard Mustang by incorporating an all-fiberglass nosepiece, and except for the bumper and headlight rims, there wasn't any other chrome on the front. The blacked-out grille had a pair of 7-inch driving lights on its extreme edges. Apart from the fenders, the entire front end was fiberglass, including the hood. This had a wide, dual inlet scoop located in the center that was functional. So were the scoops in front of the rear wheels that drew cooling air to the brakes. New too were the scoops mounted on the C-pillars that took the place of the plexiglass windows used in 1966. These scoops were also functional, extracting air from the interior. A fiberglass deck lid and spoiler finished off the attractive rear end, which was dominated by large 1967 Mercury Cougar tail lights.

See this emblem and you know you're looking at a venomous car. Shelby Mustangs eschewed the pony for this distinctive cobra badge. Note the 428 insignia; this motor was where the venom came from.

The Shelby Cobra

In many ways the Shelby Cobra, as it was called, had divorced itself from its Mustang heritage, and had become a name brand in its own right. The pony emblem had been abandoned in favor of a nest of cobras slithering out of wheel hubs, interiors, and body panels. And there was a new engine not yet shared by any Mustang, Ford's wicked 428 CJ. Rated at 335 bhp, the 428 was given high flow-heads, 10.5:1 compression ratio, and large intake and exhaust valves. Mustang's heavy duty suspension and a thicker front stabiliser bar helped give the car improved handling, but at the expense of a softer ride.

The Shelby Cobra GT500 was all muscle, and not for the faint of heart. Neither was the GT350, which continued alongside the new model. Incidentally, there were a few GT350 Cobras fitted with Paxton Super-chargers that were claimed to increase power by forty-six percent. These are exceedingly rare machines, hardly ever seen for sale.

Though in 1968 Shelby moved from being actively involved in production to the role of advisor, the Shelby Cobra of that year was still very much his design. There were three separate Cobra models for 1968: the GT350, GT500, and GT500KR. The 289 HiPo engine had been dropped in favor of the new 302 4 bbl. V-8, rated at 250 bhp. GT-500 Shelbys were given Ford's

Interceptor 428 for the first few months of 1968. It could blow the dust off most rival makes, but both the GT-500 and engine were withdrawn mid-year and replaced by the GT-500KR (King of the Road) with the 428 Cobra Jet V-8. The AGT-500KR can easily be distinguished by its side stripes advertising GT500KR just behind the front wheel well. Nineteen sixty-eight also introduced a Shelby Cobra convertible, available in all models. At year's end, a record 4,450 Shelby Cobra Mustangs had been produced, the GT500s outselling the GT350s by two to one.

The 428CJ

Chrysler, with some of the fastest cars on the block, was doing well in 1968, though its main competition was from rival big-block intermediates. But on the pony car front, Mustang was still the fastest and still king. Nevertheless, Mustang sales were considerably down compared to other pony cars, with production of only 317,404.

This 1968 Shelby GT-350 Fastback has Lucas fog lamps positioned in the grille. Note the functional scoops at the leading edge of the fiberglass hood. The rear deck lid is also fiberglass.

1968 was a year when several unique Mustangs appeared. This is the California Special made specially for California dealers to promote the marque. Hood stripes are after-market add-ons.

Brutish 1968 Shelby Mustang GT-500KR Fastback. Shelbys used a fair amount of fiberglass pieces in their construction, including the hood, which didn't always have the greatest fit.

A no nonsense
instrument panel
tells the 1968 Shelby
GT-500KR driver
all he or she needs
to know. Tach goes
to 8000 rpm, speed
a somewhat opti-
mistic 140 mph.

The 1968 Shelby
wheel replete with
cobra emblem, has
style and works well
with the GT-500KR.

FOLLOWING PAGE:
One of the best looking
Shelby Mustangs of
all, the 1968 GT-500
convertible. This car is
the GT-500KR, which
stands for "King of
the Road." And pow-
ered by Ford's awe-
some 428 Cobra Jet—
earlier models had
the 390 horse 427—
this Shelby truly
was King of the Road.

Here is the California Special's companion, the Colorado High Country Special. The beautiful setting which looks like Colorado, is actually Prescott, Arizona. Standard engine was a six-cylinder, though almost all had one of the V-8s.

In 1968, Mustang gave itself the big 428CJ engine as its top powerplant. It put out 335 bhp and, with the exception of the Shelby Cobra, was the fastest pony car around. It also produced some interesting one-year-only cars. To give Mustang a push in California and Colorado, Ford built a pair of limited edition promotional models that were sold exclusively in those states. One was the California Special, the other the High Country Special. Both cars had Shelby-like features, such as the fiber-glass rear, sequential tail lights, no pony and corral up front, Shelby-style scoops, twist-type hood locks, and British Lucas fog lamps. Mechanically, the models were identical to ordinary Mustangs and came with the 200 cid six as standard. Optional engines include the 289, 302 and 428CJ. Both models were available only as hard tops. and of the two, the High Country Special is the rarest and hardest to find.

There were other specials in 1968. To promote the new 428CJ engine, Ford introduced a special Cobra Jet Fastback. Basically a GT, the car had grille mounted fog lights and a unique GT side stripe. A wide, matte black stripe was a centerpiece of the hood, which had a functional scoop to draw cooling air onto the 428 motor nestling beneath. Another and final special in 1968 was the return of the Sprint name to promote Ford's "See The Light" sale. There were two versions of this car, a six and an eight. With the six-cylinder engine, buyers got GT stripes, pop-open gas cap, and full-wheel covers. If the buyer wanted the eight-cylinder car, all the six-cylinder items were retained, plus wide oval tires, styled steel wheels. and GT fog lamps.

Bigger and Better

During 1968, Lee Iacocca was promoted to vice-president of Ford's entire car and truck group. In this position, he no longer had the intimate relationship he'd had with the Mustang. Now he was tresponsible for much more. Semon "Bunkie" Knudsen, formerly with Pontiac, took over Iacocca's position as head of the Ford Division.

One of the first things Knudsen did was to bring in GM stylist Larry Shinoda to work on a new Mustang. Both men believed that bigger is better, and the 1969 Mustang was bigger. The 108-inch wheelbase remained as before, but four extra inches were added to the overall length. Now the car measured

The trunk of '68 High Country Special is stock Mustang, and won't hold very much. Note 1965 Thunderbird's sequential tail lights, shared with the Shelby Mustang.

The attractive High Country Special emblem, showing a golf pony galloping across a Colorado mountain range, was mounted on non-functional fiberglass side scoops.

187.4 inches bumper to bumper. The 1969 car had the most changes of all the Mustangs built over the previous five years. There were four headlights for the first time, two at the extreme edges of the grille, the other pair in the fenders. Gone was the side sculpturing, though the phony side scoop was retained, now facing rearward. The convertible and hardtop coupe had roll-down rear quarter windows, the SportsRoof—from 1969 on the fastback was given this name—had pivot windows which opened outward. The SportsRoof models had a different simulated side scoop on the rear quarter panels, just behind the door handle.

The new Mustangs offered a fresh interior. The dashboard featured two large, round pods flanked by two smaller ones, the gauges deeply recessed within the pods. The high-back bucket seats were standard and had different patterns, depending on the model. Seat belts were standard and came with shoulder harnesses.

The 1969 Mustang SportsRoof—a new name for Fastback— blends well with greenery. White outside mirrors should be green, but whitewall tires go with luxury optioned Mustangs.

The 196 grille delete bars th reappeare in 1967, afte disappea ing in 196 Bars began i 1965—seen Ford couldn make up i mind wheth to keep the or n

One of the greatest Mustangs of all, the Boss 302. The car was made to compete in the Trans Am races, where it performed very well. 302 was available only in the SportsRoof body style. The engine developed 290 bhp, and was the best handling first generation Mustang of all.

Superior Machines

Full throat-blistering power was the name of the game throughout the industry in 1969. Mustang's crop of engines started with the base 200 cid six that was joined in 1969 by a 250 cid six, developing 155 bhp. The venerable and famous 289 was replaced by the 302. In standard trim, the 302 had a 2v carburetor and developed 220 bhp. This was followed by a 2V and 4V 351 engine with delicious helpings of power. But the icing on the cake only came with the awesome 428 CJ. This engine was optional on the Mach I, which was rough, tough and ready. A pure, unadulterated street machine built to take on all comers, it had all the performance goodies, such as handling suspension, functional "Shaker" hoodscoop—that came with the 428 CJ Ram-Air engine— and dual exhausts. From its racing type hoodpins to its pop open gas cap, the Mach I was a performance machine through and through.

Actually superior in every way, and perhaps the best Mustang built until the mid-nineties, the Boss 302 was truly the one to have. Bred to race, the 302 engine with competition suspension that had staggered rearshocks, thicker front anti-roll bar, stiffer springs, a 16 to 1 steering ratio, and a 55.7% weight distribution, made for a better balanced, superior handling car. No air conditioning or automatic transmission was available for the Boss 302. It was as sporty as Mustang would ever get in those days, and could do 0–60 in 6.9 seconds. With an eye on insurance companies, Ford rated the 302 at a onservative 290 bhp, somewhat less than the 400 horses those in the know laimed the true power output to be.

One thousand units of the 302 had to be made to enable the car to qualify for he Trans Am series; actually. 1,934 were built. This was not many compared o overall Mustang production, but Ford was only interested in producing nough to homologate the potential race winner. Even fewer Mustang Boss 29 SportsRoofs were built—852 in total—but only 500 were needed to qualify or NASCAR's wide ovals. The Boss 302 won only two Trans Am events in 969, and the prospect of saying to Chevy that Mustang carried the ultimate owerplant, was probably very inviting.

Stuffing the huge V-8 into Mustang's engine bay was accomplished by nodifying the inner fender wells and the front suspension, and putting the attery into the trunk. In this way, the Boss 429 was successfuly adapted to ake the big engine. Boss 429 Mustangs, although fast—they could do 0–60 in .1 seconds—were not as fast as the Boss 302 or the Mach I. Cautiously rated t 360 bhp, it was obvious the engine put out far more than that. Besides being he most powerful, the Boss 429 was also the most expensive.

Even with all the improvements and classy new engines, Mustang sales lipped further against the opposition, chiefly the Chevy Camaro. Throw in he rest of the field, such as a superior Barracuda, Pontiac Firebird's new rans Am, AMC's Javelin, and of course, Ford's own natty Cougar XR-7, it vas fairly obvious Mustang would lose sales. The competition was very good, nd comparable in most cases to Mustang's hotter than hot new cars.

This was the time of America's unique motoring phenomenon, the brutal nuscle car. Nobody had ever seen cars quite like the Mustang, the Trans Am, r the intermediates like the Road Runner and Torino. They were the sixties ersonified, and one wondered what the seventies would bring.

Carroll Shelby was no longer involved with Shelby Mustangs by 1969. The car looked quite different from regular Mustangs. It was busy and not as handsome as pro- duction models, or Shelbys of old. The roll-bar is in deference to new safety rules.

There is nothing modified about this car. The 1970 Mustang Mach I Twister Special was built for Kansas dealers as a special promotion to help boost poor sales. Ninety-six Twisters were delivered, half with the 428 CJ V8, half with the 351 Cleveland.

CHAPTER TWO

The End of the Beginning and the Beginning of the End

If anything, 1970 was a continuation of the sixties: It was if nobody wanted to leave Woodstock and the flowers of Haight-Ashbury. The new Mustang was much the same as in 1969, though it was better looking with single headlights, a wider grille, and non-functional slots in place of fender mounted extra lights. Overall, the car had a better co-ordinated, less fussy frontal area. The adjustable rear spoiler, exclusive to the 1969 Boss 302 and 429, was available as an option on all models in 1970.

Two Specials

An interesting, though rare, Mustang model appeared in 1970. Sales were slackening across the muscle-car board. Kansas Ford dealers were particularly unhappy at the slow salesroom traffic, so they went to Ford and asked for an exclusive promotional Mustang similar to the 1968 High Country and California Specials. Ford agreed, and the result was the Twister Special. In reality a Mach I, the ninety-six Twister Specials built were painted grabber orange, had a black hood stripe, a cartoon tornado twister on the rear fenders, hood pins, and black side stripes. All the Twisters were supposed to have the savage 428 Shelby Cobra Jet V-8, but Ford ran out of powerplants after half the Twisters were built. The remaining half were given the 351 Cleveland V-8, nine of which had the four-speed manual, while the rest were equipped with the C-6 automatic. As for the 428 models, twenty-four had the manual, the remainder the automatic. All had Traction Lok limited slip differential. Kansas dealers also got ninety Torino Twisters as well. These were painted vermillion and were powered by the 429 SCJ.

Decline of the Muscle Car

In spite of the Twister, sales continued to slide in 1970. Not only Mustangs, but all muscle and pony cars were affected. Burgeoning insurance rates deterred many potential buyers, but the main reason was the public's lack of interest. Federal safety laws and exhaust emissions were slowing the cars down, as well as raising their prices. Chrysler saw the writing on the wall and closed its racing operations after 1970. Muscle cars were shortly to become as extinct as the dinosaurs.

The Boss 302 had stylish graphics which immediately identified the car as a rather special Mustang. As Ford pulled out of competition at the end of 1970, the Boss 302 was axed.

The 1970 Boss 302 was an improvement on the 1969 version. Like all 1970 Mustangs, Boss 302 returned to single headlights and a simpler, more coordinated front end. It is without a shadow of doubt, one of the best Mustangs ever built.

The rear view of the 1970 Boss was what most people saw. The triple tail light lenses on either side are actually single units.

A massive semi-hemi 429 engine is crushed into the Mustang's engine bay. Though the engine qualified to run in NASCAR competition, the Mustang didn't. NASCAR wouldn't entertain ponies—only interme- diates and larger—so the engine ran in Torinos for the most part.

1971 gave birth to
Larry Shinoda's big
Mustang. Actually
it was only 2.1 inches
longer and 2.4 inches
wider. The styling
created an optical
illusion, making it
appear much bigger.

The Mach I Sportsroof in-
terior like the exterior
appears larger and
roomier than previous
Mustangs, whereas the
actual size difference is
quite small.

Bunkie Knudsen and stylist Larry Shinoda continued to reshape the Mustang. Knudsen and Shinoda's preference for big cars was apparent in the 1971 Mustangs he designed, which were bigger, wider, and heavier—or they appeared to be. In fact, they were only 2.1 inches longer and 2.4 inches wider. What Shinoda created was an illusion; clever styling, such as a new SportsRoof design with an almost flat—and useless—rear window, made the cars look as long as a battleship.

It was once predicted that the Seventies would be the "Sizzlin' Seventies," and Mustang would be emphasizing performance more than ever. Unfortunately, exactly the opposite happened. Like Chrysler, Ford pulled out of racing, after ten years of sweet success in motoring competition. The reason was Ford's reaction to growing public concerns about safety, emissions, and economy, and the effect these views were having on the government. Plans were afoot for a complete change of Mustang's image. Hardly had the 1971 Mustangs been earmarked for production, than Henry Ford II summoned Bunkie Knudsen to his office and dismissed him. Shortly after that, Larry Shinoda resigned in protest.

Iacocca Returns

It was back to Lee Iacocca, who had let it be known that he didn't care for the Knudsen/Shinoda Mustang. In fact, he was downright angry. Shortly after resuming direction of Mustang, he headed for Italy and the Ghia design studio, where he explained that he wanted to return to Mustang's original concept. Iacocca predicted the decline of the muscle car, given the high insurance rates for powerful vehicles and the threat of an oil shortage on the horizon.

A rear view of the 1971 SportsRoof shows off the nearly flat window that was almost impossible to see out of, especially if the driver was short. The engine was the Boss 351 Ram-Air, a high compression, high output Cleveland unit that really made the Mach I move.

The Boss 351 came with a "Shaker" functional hood scoop. The hood stripes denote the car is a 351.

His misgivings proved correct; 1971 Mustang sales crashed to 149,678 units. The message was clear: The public wanted sensible cars again. Two months after Iacocca's visit to Italy, Ghia delivered to Ford what would be the basis for the new Mustang. Introduction for the Mustang II, as it would be called, was set for 1974. There was nothing Iacocca could do with the existing model, which was locked in for three seasons. Ford would have to hope the car could hold its own until 1974.

As always with Mustang, the 1971 line-up contained a couple of specialty models. The Boss 351 succeeded the now deleted Boss 302 and Boss 429. The Cleveland 351 had been introduced in 1970 to replace the Windsor 351 V-8. The Cleveland had canted valves and 330 horsepower and was definitely fast. Hence, the engine's promotion to become the powerhouse behind the Boss 351. Equipped with Ram-Air, solid lifters, an aluminum intake manifold, and four-barrel carburetors, the Boss 351 kept Mustang's image going with 0–60 times of 5.8 seconds. Then there was the Mach I, which could be ordered with a docile 2 bbl 302, or the rip roaring semi-hemi 429.

An overhead view of the rare Boss 351 convertible with its top up. Very few were made of this car that made its official debut in 1971.

FOLLOWING PAGE: Shown driving across an old Indiana bridge is the most savage Mustang of all, the Boss 429. To accomodate the extra wide powerplant, engineers had to move the spring towers out an inch on either side. And to compensate for the nose-heavy weight, the A-arms were lowered one inch. All this to homologate the engine for NASCAR.

Another 1971 Boss 351 Ram-Air powered Mach I. The different flat black motif on hood and concealed windshield wipers were new for 1971.

1970 was a good year for high performance Mustangs. There was the Boss 302, Boss 429, Mach I, the Shelby, and the Boss 351. This was a rare addition to the fleet, and wasn't truly recognized for what it was until much later.

Here's another modified, English owned 1970 Mach I. It has a unique paint job and sexy art on the hood. The functional "Shaker" came standard with the 428 engine. Mustangs are very popular and desirable in the UK.

A worm's-eye view of the 1970 Mustang Mach I SportsRoof captures the aggressive look of the model with its modified paint-job.

The traditional leftward galloping pony graces the Boss 302 grille, as it does on all 1970 Mustang models.

Ford used the Sprint name for the last time in 1972 to make a patriotic red, white, and blue hardtop and SportsRoof. There's even a USA shield emblem on the rear fender. Some Pintos and Mavericks shared the same color schemes in 1972.

New parking/turn signal lights differentiate the 1973 Mustang Mach I SportsRoof from its 1971–72 counterparts. An additional couple of inches were added to the overall length, making the 1973 model the largest Mustangs of all time.

The 1973 Mustang was longer, due to the Federal Government's five-mile-per-hour frontal impact bumpers. Behind the urethane is a steel bar, an impact beam, and a pair of absorbers. If hit, the bumper moves back on the energy absorbers, then bounces back, hopefully intact.

With muscle cars on their way out, Mustang's 1972 series had only the Mach I to hold the performance banner aloft. It featured a color-keyed, urethane front bumper, which had become popular when it was introduced in 1971. In February 1972, Ford introduced the Sprint, a handsome car that was produced for one year only. Overall production for all Mustangs in 1972 fell to 125,093—the lowest number yet.

The final year of the Shinoda Mustang was 1973, which ended its run with a more pronounced eggcrate grille and vertical parking lamps. It was also the largest Mustang of all time, measuring 194 inches. This was not entirely the stylists' fault; the government required all cars to have 5 mph impact bumpers from 1973 on, and it was these that added the extra length. As before, there was a choice of three: the coupe, SportsRoof, and convertible. Standard Mach I engine was the 302 two- barrel V-8, but there was still a 351 two-barrel sporting Ram-Induction.

For a more accurate guide to horsepower, Mustangs were switched to the European net figures. Net tells the horsepower when the engine has all the accessories, while gross horsepower counts only the engine block. For example, a 330 bhp (gross) became 275 bhp (net). Production rose to 134,267 in 1973.

The attractive galloping pony gas cap is positioned in the center of the rear panel.

The huge hood emphasizes the 1973 Mustang's length: at least seven feet long. There were five engines for a buyer to choose from for this smart convertible, starting with the 250 cid six, up to the high performance 351 Cobra-Jet.

This 1973 Mustang had the 351 Ram-Air V8 under its long hood. Though not a patch on earlier Mustangs when it came to performance, this final first generation Mustang could still dig in its heels and fly.

The full frontal of the 1972 Mustang Sprint shows off its nicely done red, white, and blue colors. Note that the red is thin line framing the blue stripes

This was the stock, four-cylinder powered 1976 Mustang II. Condemned in 1974 as a "souped up Pinto," the little car was treated like the ugly duckling of the car world. In its favor was far better workmanship than found on first generation models, and superior quality interior materials.

The Second Generation

By midsummer 1973, first generation Mustang production came to an end, as Ford factories switched over to the second generation cars. The rumors of a considerably smaller Mustang to come were well founded. In his meetings with Ghia, Iacocca had insisted on a 100-inch wheelbase, sporty looks, shorter length, a four-speed manual transmission, and a four-cylinder engine as standard. Borrowing elements from the Pinto, Falcon, and Fairlaine, the 175-inch Mustang was offered in two body styles: the luxury Ghia coupe and a vinyl-roof hatchback. Unfortuantely, the OHC four-cylinder, 140 cid engine, developing 88 bhp (net), was slow to accelerate.

Though there was heavy criticism from the motoring press ("Mustang II... is about as close to a sports car as a Sherman tank."), the 1974 Mustang sold. The oil crisis had begun in October 1973, creating high fuel costs and long gas lines, and people were no longer in the mood for the automotive blood 'n' guts days of yore. The little Mustang was cute enough to win approval from a

From the sublime to the ridiculous, the 1974 Mustang II. The motoring press hated the car, but the public went for it, four cylinders and all. To be fair, the car's introduction was perfectly timed, coming out just as the oil crisis worsened.

Mustang II was heavily critcized and served as a transitional model. Sold for only four years, it was replaced in 1979 by the third generation Mustangs.

At least the rear window returned to good sense in the Mustang II; one didn't have to be seven feet tall to look out of it, anymore. The car isn't all that bad looking from the rear and actually has sensible amber turn signals.

To try and inject a little life into the Mustang II, a Cobra II debuted in 1976. More show than go, the Cobra II offered an emissions strangled 302 V-8, putting out 139 bhp (SAE net).

Encouraged by this, and with the oil crisis ending, Ford offered the 302 V-8 n the 1975 Mustang. Strangled with emissions, low compression, and a dismal 34 bhp (net), the V-8 was hard put to achieve 60 mph in under 11 seconds. rue, it was better than the four-cylinder's 17 seconds, but the cost was a high uel bill. Even with all the restrictions, the Mustang II had to live with, Ford ngineers and stylists tried their utmost to make something of the little car. here was a Mach I version powered by the V-6 as standard, but with 1975 roduction dipping to 188,575, something had to be done for 1976. That some- hing was the Cobra II, all flash with spoilers, racing stripes, handling suspen- ion, and the 302, developing 139 bhp. The car was better than the average Mustang II, and was beautifully put together. Iacocca was adamant that uality was number one, and that the materials used should be the best.

"Humpy and Dumpy",
Road & Track called
it, but the Mustang II's
initial sales figures told
a different story. This
is the 1975 Mach I, which
had a 171-cid, German
built V-6 as standard.
The 302 V-8 was an option.

The ugly duckling tried a bunch of go-faster spoilers, valences, orange wheels and T-tops in 1978, when the King Cobra was introduced. The car had performance suspension, quicker steering and the 302 V-8. The King Cobra could do the quarter-mile in 17 seconds.

Recapturing the Glory

As it became clear that the Mustang II would not be a long term success, the decision was made in 1976 to build an all new Mustang in the hope it might recapture the magic of 1964–1973. Once again FoMoCo's various design studios competed with each other to see who would come up with the winning entry. As it turned out, the final design was a composite of elements from several entries. One model had an interesting front, another a good roof line and so on. All the best elements were then blended into one cohesive design. Once everyone saw the final model, they knew they had found the third generation Mustang.

In 1978, Mustang II's final year, a striking new model was offered. This was the King Cobra, a paint-on, performance package that was impressive, if somewhat garish, with an array of features and a black glass T-Top. It offered halfway decent handling, faster rack and pinion steering than usually employed, a plastic, brushed aluminum-style dashboard, and a sporty, racing type steering wheel. The car tried to kid the world that it was a true sports machine, but it wasn't. Still, it was better than the standard offerings, in spite of the splattered cartoon cobra splayed across the hood. Not too many King Cobras were made, so it is quite rare and desirable for collectors who like something a little different.

If nothing else, the Mustang II served as a transitional car until better days returned, and its four years were instantly forgotten when Ford unveiled the 1979 third generation models. Here was a car that made sense, had style, and looked as though it had sporting promise. Since aerodynamics were beginning to play a part in car design to achieve fuel economy, Ford made use of wind tunnels in planning the 1979 Mustang. One hundred thirty-six hours of wind tunnel testing produced a drag co-efficient of 0.46 for the coupe, 0.44 for the fastback. The third generation Mustang was obviously moving in the right direction.

At a time when car designers seem to have lost their way, the new Mustang was the beginning of the road back to former glory. Although the 1979 Mustang had an entirely different body, the engine line up was the same. The four developed 88 bhp, the V-6 109 bhp, and the 302 V-8 140 bhp. An interesting innovation was the optional turbo-charger to boost the four-cylinder engine's performance. Road tests using the turbo-charged four, recorded 0–60 times of about 11.5 seconds. While aerodynamics had been used to aid in the design of the new car, the Mustang's shape was sharper, squarer, and definitely European.

Fenders were still bolt-on affairs in 1978, thus making them far easier to replace than welded ones. The venerable 302 fits neatly under the hood, though there's not much room to work on the engine.

"Basket handle" roll bar helps keep T-tops in place on King Cobra. Made for one season only, the King Cobra is by far the most desirable Mustang II of all, and is actively sought after by collectors.

*After four years the
Mustang II was gone.
It sold reasonably
well and has become
a bit of a cult object
in collector circles.
Its replacement was
the 1979 third generation
Mustang, and had heavy
European influence.*

Only two models, a hatchback and a notchback (coupe), were available in various trim levels. If a buyer wanted luxury, then it was the Ghia, and seat of the pants enthusiasts could opt for the Cobra. In 1979, there was a special limited edition Indy 500 model, since the Mustang had been picked to pace the great race. At 179.1 inches overall, the 1979 Mustang was two inches shorter than the 1965 first generation car, yet five inches longer than the Mustang II. Wheel base grew from 92 inches to 100 inches, which was eight inches shorter than the original. Furthermore, the 1979 options list was longer than ever. There was a flip-up glass sunroof, remote trunk release, leather upholstery, numerous wheels, radio systems, power everything, T-tops, and much more.

Production of the new Mustang soared to 332,025 units in 1979. Considering the American double-digit inflation rate, Mustang sales were a touch of the

No longer a King but still a Cobra, this 1979 model had the 5.0L V-8, which was now peppy enough to zip to 60 mph in 9.0 seconds. Apart from the silly looking squashed Cobra on the hood, the car was very definitely in the European mode.

sun in an otherwise leaden sky. In spite of this, Henry Ford II suddenly fired Iacocca. Reasons were never given for this, but there is a probability that Iacocca didn't fit into Ford's social circle. Iacocca was a tell-it-like-it-is kind of guy, straight-forward, and unpretentious. Perhaps Iacocca's familiarity rankled Ford; obviously to him class meant more than results.

Though 1980 was the beginning of a decade of profound change, nothing much was happening on the car front. Though Detroit had begun to make positive moves to make the American automobile as up-to-date as the hot selling Japanese cars, Mustang changed little in 1980. Only the Cobra received minor alterations in the form of a new hood scoop, grille, and different go-faster stripes. The 302 cid V-8 was dropped to be replaced by a 255 cid engine. This was a bored out version of the old 1962 Fairlane 221 unit that had served Ford well over the years. Rated at 117 bhp (net) the engine wasn't as quick as the 302 but served CAFE (Corporate Average Fuel Economy) regulations for a few years.

After abandoning sporting activities in 1970, Ford made a welcome come-back in September 1980 with the formation of the Special Vehicles Operations unit. This would result in the building of special Mustangs to race in Trans Am and Imsa competitions. Two hundred fifty very desirable McLaren Mustangs were also built and priced at $25,000 per car, quite a lot when compared to $6000 for a fully equipped standard machine.

FOLLOWING PAGE: Tooling down a wintry road at dusk, this 1989 Mustang is a much modified car built by SAAC. Although the body remains unaltered, the suspension is lowered and engine power tweaked with the healthy result of superior performance and handling.

Quicker than you think, Mustang's twentieth anniversary rolled around in 1984. To celebrate the auspicious occasion, Mustang treated everybody to the GT 350—the T-top version is shown here. The car was replete with goodies, but the Euro influence was still strong.

The Eighties

Times were bad in the early eighties as America sank into recession. Car sales declined considerably in 1980, with Mustang down 90,000 units over 1979. At the same time, car prices were steadily rising. Between 1976 and 1986, the price of a Mustang climbed from $4,047 to almost $11,000, and by 1989 some models cost $18,000. In 1982, 130,418 Mustangs were produced, followed by a new production low in 1983 when only 120,873 were made.

The time when American automobiles underwent annual changes, sometimes drastic ones, was past. A new car in 1979 might remain the same for years. This was cetainly true of the Mustang, which was hardly altered for fourteen years, keeping costs down and profits up. Of course, there were some changes: a new High Output 302 V-8 came in 1982 with considerably improved acceleration. It clocked zero to sixty in eight seconds. Body changes to the '82 Mustags were minimal—only a new front end. A 302 (5 liter) powered GT model replaced the Cobra, which was laid to rest.

Nineteen eighty-three Mustangs, in keeping with the new aerodynamic fashion, had a rounder nose section, which was barely noticeable. Another old soldier died that year, when the venerable straight six was repleced by a lightweight V-6. A better performer and more frugal with gas, the new engine became Mustang's base motor.

Finally, in 1984, the economy began to improve and car sales began an upward climb. Mustang production rose to 141,480 units in a year when a pair on interesting models were launched. One was the GT350 which was hyped as a twentieth anniversary model. Available in fastback (with T-tops) or convertible form, the limited edition GT350 was painted in white only, with red trim and interior. Powered by the HO 302 (5.0L) V-8, the GT350 was quite a car.

The Cobra was gone by 1982,
slithering off into the sunset.
It was replaced by the excellent
Mustang GT three-door hatchback
coupe. Under the hood was the
302 (5.0L) Hi-Po V-8. Traction
Loc limited slip differential and
handling suspension were part
of the performance package.

The 1984 5.0L GT would have
been equally at home on Germany's
Autobahn, as well as an American
interstate. It was quick, but
European technology was more
advanced, thus allowing BMWs
and Audis to fly past at will.

The SVO

Far more important, however, was the introduction of the Mustang SVO. As the SVO letters imply, it was put together by the Special Vehicles Operations team. As a truly sporting grand tourer with rapid acceleration and road handling, the SVO was by far the best Mustang to date. Powered by a throttle-body, fuel-injected -V-8 engined GT. The little four zoomed from 0–60 in 7.5 seconds, and had a top speed of 130 mph. The SVO had all the technological goodies currently available; four-wheel disc brakes, adjustable shock absorbers, five-speed manual transmission, performance suspension, and rack and pinion steering. 225/50VR-16 Goodyear NCT radial tires were mounted on 7-inch wide aluminum wheels. Articulated Recaro- type leather seats with lumbar support were part of the very European interior—in fact the whole car was more European than American. Flared wheel arches, a large and functional hood scoop, twin rear spoilers, and the first Mustang not to have a grille, the SVO cost a whopping $16,000 or more. First the price, then the American love for V-8 power probably discouraged many from buying this, the best of all Mustangs at the time.

Out of a 1984 production total of 140,480 units, only 4,508 of them were SVOs. In 1985, a mere 1,954 SVOs sold, and 3,382 in 1986, the SVO's last year in production. Special Vehicles shoveled the turbo-four and all that went with it, into the new Thunderbird. This didn't last long either, but it was a great car, nevertheless.

Mustang's SVO was by far the best of the marque to come down the turnpike. Now the Europeans faced a machine that was much harder to beat. Its turbo-charged, 140-cid sohc four-cylinder engine could do zero to sixty in 7 seconds and had a top speed approaching 140 mph. This is the 1985 model.

Apart from the excitement surrounding the SVO, Mustang plodded through the eighties and early nineties evolving, modifying, and perfecting an already good car. Three body styles were used: the three-door coupe (hatchback), the two-door coupe, and the convertible. There were variations on two basic models, the LX and GT. The least expensive Mustang in 1986 was the LX two-door coupe at $7,189. This had the four-cylinder engine as standard. The V-8 was standard with the GT series. Highest priced Mustang was the GT convertible at $14,523. The inflated prices didn't put people off; the recession was over, the public was buying again, and, as a result, Mustang production increased to 224,410 units in 1986.

225 bhp from its 5.0L V-8 helped the 1987 Mustang convertible along the road at more than double the speed limit, if anyone was foolish enough to try. A nod to aerodynamics can be seen by the soft-ening of the front end.

An Uncertain Future

Perhaps the increase in monthly payments inhibited sales in 1987, for Mustang production dropped 70,000 units over 1986. Or perhaps the eight-year-old body was becoming a little dated, especially when compared to Ford's state-of-the-art Taurus. Ford had taken a leap forward in design, and the Taurus and

Here's the 5.0L V-8 in all its glory. Note the fuel injection and the critical lack of space to work on the engine. One cannot even see the spark plugs, let alone get at them.

its sister car the Mercury Sable, were the highpoints in automobile fashion. However, though many people wanted these cars, America's most popular automobile was the Honda Accord.

When rumors circulated that Ford was seriously thinking of dropping the Mustang and replacing it with a smaller, lighter Mazda-based sporty car, thousands of letters arrived at Ford headquarters pleading for the Mustang to remain as it was. This car was as American as the Stars and Stripes, and nobody wanted it changed into a front-wheel drive Japanese sportscar. Ford relented and promised to continue the Mustang as before, renaming the Mazda-based car the Probe.

Nineteen eighty-nine was the tenth anniversary of the Mustang body and frame that Ford was determined to continue for a few more years. The major worry was—what then? The Probe had proved a success in its own right, and Ford began to wonder whether a brand new Mustang would be worth the financial commitment. All the talk at Ford was about the fate of the Mustang, forgetting that it was the pony's twenty-fith anniversary. Dealers and the public expected a special limited edition car, but when none was forthcoming, uncertainty grew in peoples' minds. Was this a sign that Ford was going to put the Mustang out to grass?

The 1989 Mustang GT 5.0L convertible is virtually identical to the 1987–88 models. Ford used the same body and FOX frame from 1979 thru 1993. Simpler LX design didn't have machismo look, but was just as fast with the 5.0L engine.

Here's the 1984 twentieth anniversary GT 350 convertible. Carroll Shelby took umbrage when he discovered Ford was using his GT-350 title, and issued a cease-and-desist order. This effectively prevented further use of the title, but not before the 1984 season ended.

*Mustang 5.0L convertible was what you got to
go cruising on hot Friday summer nights in 1992.*

CHAPTER THREE

Wow! That's Something Else

By 1989 the ten-year-old body was getting a spread; especially the GT which was covered in scoops, spoilers, and ground effects. More rounded, with flush headlights and color-keyed bumpers, the GT's 5.0L V-8 delivered the right noises to delight the macho element. The car's look projected machismo, albeit the overweight variety reminiscent of those large hell's angels of times gone by. In contrast, the LX was quite attractive and every bit as fast, if equipped with the V-8 engine.

Another Redesign

A group of engineers, designers, and marketing men formed to discuss the car's problems, and decided that a new Mustang could be designed and built for far less money than originally supposed. To do this. a "collocated/dedicated" team would need their on building, and think and work only on the Mustang, without being involved in other projects. This was approved and work began.

Meanwhile, in response to the flagging sales of 1990, Ford brought out a L limited edition Mustang convertible painted Emerald Jewel Green Metallic Clearcoat. It had a white top and white leather interior, and cost $19,878. Only 3,837 were built. Once again, America was dipping into recession, and 1991 Mustang production took another slide, despite new 16-inch alloy wheels and a more gutsy 2.3L four-cylinder engine boasting two spark plugs per cylinder. Thanks to the new cylinder head, horsepower was boosted from 88 to 105.

For 1992 Ford put out another limited edition. This one was painted Vibrant Red, and had a white top with ebony headliner. Opal pearlescent 16-inch wheels, unique rear-deck spoiler, and white leather interior set the car apart. In spite of these features, a mere 2,196 were sold.

Getting ready to drag at Michigan's Milan Raceway, this 1991/92 5.0L has been nursed and coddled to the point that straight line acceleration is something Ford engineers could only wish to deliver.

As the 1993 Mustangs hit the streets, the mini-recession was ending. Production moved up to 96,225 for the year, and included a couple of interesting models for the final season of the old body style. There were two limited edition models: one all white with matching white leather seats, and a striking yellow car with either black or white leather interiors. These specials had the traditional Mustang pony embroidered on the seats. Both models were powered by the 5.0L, which suffered a horsepower reduction from 225 bhp to 205. Production was limited to 1,419 yellow models and 1,460 white ones.

The SVT

In 1993 Special Vehicle Operations was renamed Special Vehicles Team, and in midyear SVT brought out a new Cobra, the first for a number of years. Fitted out with the usual compliment of spoilers and ground effects, the new Cobra was certainly one of the better Mustang variations. It was loaded to the gills, and handled and drove like a thoroughbred. It had 17-inch wheels and special performance suspension. Under the hood, the five-liter engine had GT40-style cylinder heads, a different camshaft, and to allow the cam more lift, 1.7:1-ratio rocker arms. Horsepower was conservatively rated at 235, though 270 was nearer the truth. In roadtest comparisons between the Cobra and the brand new Camaro Z/28, boasting a 40 hp advantage, Cobra came out on top every time. Every one of the 4,993 Cobras built were sold.

Limited Edition LX model had exotic chrome wheels, a fad that took off with cars that were regarded as special. The wheels were not available on standard Mustangs.

A total of 1,419 yellow Limited Edition 5.0L Mustangs were built. Top quality materials were used and the car was striking. There was a white model, too; they produced 1,460 of that on

1993 was the last yea of the 1979 body style a new Mustang was the wings. Ford gave th elderly design a grea send-off with variou limited editions and sparkling new Cobr Here is one of the limite editions, given a stripe bumble bee appearan by noontime shadou

However, there was an even tougher Cobra put together by SVT. This was the Cobra R, a pure, no-holds-barred racing car. There was no sound deadening, no radio, and no rear seat. There was no compliance in the ride; it was as hard as bouncing about on a bed of nails, and had all the right stuff to go racing. Unfortunately, very few ever saw a race track, because most of the 107 built were snapped up by speculators, hoping to turn their $25,217 investment into a quick profit.

The Mustang III

By the middle of 1993, the general public knew a new Mustang was in the wings. A lot of magazine copy was given to the Mustang III show car. It was a convertible, very aerodynamic, had a "chopped" windshield and two seats. Under the hood was Ford's 4.6-liter overhead cam modular V-8. A wonderful looking car, but one that was not about to happen, even though there were teasing similarities between the new Mustang and the show car. The world would have to wait until almost Christmas to see how close the similarities were.

This rear view of the 1991 car shows integrated spoilers and interesting tail light design. It only lasted a couple of seasons.

Talk about aerodynamic! This is the 1993 Mustang III Concept Car that Ford heavily publicized, dropping hints here and there that maybe, just maybe, some of the Mustang III elements would end up in the new model.

The 1991 Mustang 5.0L was no different than the 1990 version, or 1989 for that matter. Sales took a nose dive in the year of President Bush's Gulf War—whether the shorter than short conflict had anything to do with low sales is anybody's guess.

Another road hugging view of the Mustang III. According to the under-hood wording, the car was the Mach III as well. Mustang III was a full working model powered by Ford's DOHC V-8 rated at a staggering 450 horsepower. It had 19-inch wheels, Roots type blower, and a six-speed transmission.

Finally, 1994 arrived and so did the new Mustang. It was totally different, yet retained the old, but much altered FOX frame and the venerable 5.0L V-8. This has the eight-cylinder OHV engine.

This leather-seated interior is attractive and well finished. There's not a great deal of room at the rear, but cars of this nature aren't meant to be family carry-alls. This is a car for the young and young at heart, and more than two people would be too many.

You will notice that all modern cars have engines that are almost totally inaccessible. This is to make sure you have to take the car to a dealer to be worked on, thereby costing you a lot of money for a simple job like changing spark plugs.

As for the 1993 Mustang, the Cobra was the last hurrah for a fourteen-year-old design. Car enthusiasts everywhere waited with bated breath for Mustang's fourth generation car. It was developed under a revolutionary new program called World Class Timing, in which each part of the process was broken into segments— such as design, engineering, marketing, and so on— and every element of the development was carefully reviewed and discussed by the team that worked together under one roof. By the time the car was complete, it had been designed and built in 35 months—eight weeks ahead of schedule—and at a cost of $700 million, a saving of 30% over the traditional way of doing things.

Although the 1994 Mustang looked all new and radical, it wasn't entirely. As the team developed the car, they realized they could modify and use the old Fox platform. Christened FOX-4, the new/old platform was strengthened and stiffened without compromising ride or comfort. Considering the car used the traditional front engine, rear drive design, it had handling and ride never thought possible with what might be termed an antiquated live rear-axle system. A new 3.8L V-6, developing 145 bhp, replaced the four-cylinder unit that had been in service as base engine since 1974.

The V-6 had been around for some time and was used in the Continental and Taurus automobiles. Sequential port fuel-injection and a new EEC-V engine management system aided economy and efficiency. Even in these days when there are hardly any V-8 powerplants anymore, the desire to own an eight-cylinder powered car is still very strong. A Mustang without a V-8 was unthinkable, something that could never happen. Nobody needed to have worried; there was a V-8, a lineal descendant of the 302 (5.0L) previously used. Because the new Mustang's shape was so different, the normal 5.0L wouldn't fit, so it was decided to use the modified unit that powered the Thunderbird and Cougar. This engine fitted neatly under the Mustang's hood after the engineers moved it forward 0.75 of an inch to accomodate the "four into two" catalytic converters. Moving it forward only slightly meant there was no room for the radiator cooling fan. The answer was an electric fan that had the advantage of not taking horsepower from the engine. Suspension consisted of a modified MacPherson strut system up front with the coil springs placed between the front crossmember and lower control arms, which were longer to improve steering and suspension geometries. Directional stability was improved by increasing the front caster from 1.5 to 4 degrees. At the rear, the ancient rigid axle had been lifted intact from the '93 model. It was located by four trailing links and the coil springs were placed between the body and lower links. There were four shock absorbers: two placed normally and two horizontally to prevent axle wind-up. Anti-roll bars, front and rear, were standard on all models. There was no hatchback in the model line-up, only a coupe and convertible. Ford claimed it couldn't build a hatchback with sufficient structural rigidity, even though the Japanese were exporting similar cars as hatchbacks at two thirds the price of the Mustang.

FOLLOWING PAGE: Amid a fair amount of ballyhoo, the 1994 fourth generation Mustang made its appearance. This is FoMoCo's picture of the new 5.0L GT coupe.

One of the first 1994 Mustangs to hit the streets, this car is seen on a chilly November day in 1993. Mustang has standard 3.8L, 145 horse V-6 under the hood. The horse alongside is a real Mustang, by the way.

Selling the New Car

When the new car was unveiled on December 8, 1993, there wasn't the pandemonium that had greeted the original Mustang, even though there was almost as much hype as there had been thirty years before. The car was previewed in a hundred cities before it went on sale. Working with the various Mustang clubs across the country, Ford put together Mustang parties in major venues to gauge consumer's reactions. Overall, they liked the new Mustang. Very rounded and aerodynamic, the car gracefully showed its lineage. The side indentation and scoop alluded to the past, as did the long hood and short rear. A small, half-oval-shaped, open grille graced the front with the leftward galloping pony in the center. An estimated 137,000 Mustang 1994 models were produced, some 41,000 more than the previous year.

There was no change to the standard Mustang in 1995, but in 1996 the 5.0 OHV engine was replaced by Ford's 4.6L modular overhead cam V-8. It put out 190 horses in standard form, 210 with the optional dual exhausts. Although the engine was very smooth in operation its long stroke configuration lessened low-end torque to the point that it didn't have the muscle car punch of old. To try and help matters, Ford added five extra horses in 1997 to bring the GT engine up to 215.

In response to criticism about performance, Ford pushed the GT Mustang's horsepower up to 225 for 1998. This brought a minor improvement in acceleration and top speed, though the GT is still no match for the Camaro Z-28 in performance terms.

Fluffy white clouds, wafting across a bright blue summer sky, are reflected in the new purple clearcoat color given to this 1996 Mustang GT convertible. Under the hood was Ford's modular V-8 pumping out 215 bhp.

A 1995 Mustang GT Special Sports Edition convertible probably had something to do with Mustang's thirtieth anniversary. It had the 5.0L 215 horsepower motor and handling suspension.

A bare bones interior was all the buyer got with the Cobra-R. It was not meant for the street, and was sold only to genuine racing concerns.

Here was the ultimate Mustang, the mighty Cobra-R. Built by Special Vehicles Team, the Cobra-R was for racing only. There was no rear seat and the minimum of accessories. Only 240 were made.

The Cobra in the Nineties

In 1995 there was a new Cobra-R. Built entirely for racing purposes, Ford allowed only 240 to be made, and would only accept orders from bonafide racecar organizations. However, when Ford found, as it did in 1993, that the cars were being sold to collectors and speculators. it was the end of Cobra-R. A bare bones coupe without rear seat, radio, or air, the Cobra-R employed not the familiar 5.0L OH V-8, but was given the whopping 351 (5.8L) engine. In the few events in which the Cobra-R competed, it proved faster than rival Camaro Z-28s in the same races. But that was the end of both the Cobra-R and the 5.0L V-8, Mustang's standard engine since the beginning. From 1996 on, the Cobra SVT would have Ford's successful modular overhead cam V-8, though with differences not shared in other Fords using the same engine. For one thing, the modular V-8 changes its spots in the Cobra, altering from single overhead cam to double overhead cam with four valves per cylinder. This 32-valve engine is unique, because Ford uses international technology to produce one of the world's best motors. The Cobra's aluminum alloy block and heads are cast in Italy, and the steel crankshaft is forged in Germany. Then, the parts are shipped to Ford's Romeo, Michigan engine plant where the Cobra engines are hand-assembled. The finished 4.6-liter engine has a compression ratio of 9.85:1, and develops 305 hp at 5800 rpm. Even though the Cobra isn't quite as fast—155 mph compared to the Camaro Z-28's 163—it has superior ride quality without sacrificing very refined handling.

The front suspension is independent, having a modified MacPherson-type design with a unique 9mm stabilizer bar. At the rear, the suspension follows Ford's QuadraLink principles with an outboard trailing arm supporting the spring near its midpoint, and the axle near its end. A 27mm stabilizer bar links the two lower trailing arms, running behind and below the rear axle. Inboard upper trailing arms extend from the body structure to attachment points near the differential housing. The shock absorbers are vertical, standing behind the axle. Horizontally mounted hydraulic leading links aid in locating the axle and reduce fore-aft movement and wheelhop during savage acceleration.

The heart of the matter. Under the Cobra-R's hood lay 5.8 liters of pure venom. The big OHV V-8 developed 300 bhp. at 4800 rpm. In 1996 this engine was put out to grass, and Ford's 4 cam, 4.6L replaced the traditional 5.0 V-8. There were no more Cobra R racing cars after 1995.

Shown here are two new colors offered on the Cobra SVT in 1998. Power remains the 32 valve 4.6 liter V-8 that develops 305 bhp. Each Cobra engine is hand assembled by one of a dozen two- person teams, and a small plate is attached to the engine, engraved with the signatures of the pair who built it. A touch of class, indeed.

This then, has been the Mustang-Cobra since 1996. It is not perfect, but then, what car is? Taking into account the old live rear axle, the SVT people have done a remarkable job in making the Cobra as good as it is. There are one or two things that could be done to really make the Cobra howl. Having driven the 1998 version, it is obvious that the engine needs a little more pep. The five-speed gearbox is very good with close ratios, but first and second could do with some help. Before one even starts to mash the right foot in first or second, one finds a change down is required. Power appears to come on in third and fourth gears when the climb to the red line limit is not quite as rapid. Rough roads also cause the Cobra to get out of sorts, which indicates a good independent rear suspension is called for. Overall, a good car despite everything.

Looking Ahead

What does the future hold for America's favorite pony car as we cross the bridge into the twenty-first century? Nobody's saying at the moment, but there is little doubt the Mustang will remain a front engine, rear drive automobile. However, the hope and likelihood is for an independent rear suspension system that will finally make the Mustang as advanced and as good as anything produced in the world. Now that Chrysler and Mercedes have become one, it goes without saying that there are going to be technical marvels coming out of Auburn Hills in the the not too distant future. Ford, with its huge European operations and experience, its ownership of Jaguar and Aston Martin, can beat everyone to the punch with a Mustang to end all Mustangs. As a world-class automobile, the Mustang is almost there. Give the engine a bit more torque, a six-speed box instead of the the current Borg-Warner T-5 five-speed, plus the aforementioned independent rear suspension, and the public's love affair with the Mustang will start all over again. Only this time, it will be the Ultimate Mustang.